John Cussons

A Glance at Current History

John Cussons

A Glance at Current History

ISBN/EAN: 9783743399716

Manufactured in Europe, USA, Canada, Australia, Japa

Cover: Foto ©ninafisch / pixelio.de

Manufactured and distributed by brebook publishing software (www.brebook.com)

John Cussons

A Glance at Current History

A GLANCE

AT

CURRENT HISTORY

BY

JOHN CUSSONS,

Past-Grand Commander of the Confederate Veterans of Virginia;
Ex-Chairman of History Committee, &c.

GLEN ALLEN, VA.
CUSSONS, MAY & COMPANY, INC.
1899.

TO THE MEMORY OF
MY COMRADES
WHO FELL IN DEFENCE
OF THEIR
INHERITED LIBERTIES
THESE PAGES ARE
AFFECTIONATELY INSCRIBED.

Publishers' Note.

These pages give the candid utterances of a Confederate soldier who strenously opposed disunion; not as doubting the rightfulness of secession, but as gravely questioning its expediency.

During the period of agitation which preceded the war he believed that the revolutionary spirit which then infected the North was but a passing phase of fanaticism, and that that fanaticism was destined to perish under the rebuke of all good citizens who, he believed, would surely unite in upholding the Constitution and the laws. But when Lincoln's call for an army of invasion found so swift response among the multitude, it became evident that Northern conservatism had been over-estimated, and that the advocates of secession had really read the portents aright.

The author has always held that the full measure of America's greatness could be achieved only beneath a single flag, but he is equally firm in the conviction that a true spirit of national unity will never be attained by a distortion of historic truths. He believes that the highest and noblest aspirations of a people will take their impress from that which is worthiest in their traditions, and that if they are so unfortunate as to feel no just pride in their past they may well despair of finding any rational hope for their future. In short, he insists that there can be no evil so deep and abiding as that which must befall a people who have been taught to hold the memory of their ancestors in derision and contempt. Believing thus, his creed is: "Absolute fairness in the historic treatment of the past, and then unity of effort for the upbuilding of a nation such as the world has not seen."

CONTENTS.

		PAGE
I.	A Glance at Current History,	11
II.	On History as Taught in Our Schools,	77
III.	On "Teachable" History,	89
IV.	On the Outworn Theory of Government by Consent,	113
V.	On Granting Forgiveness Before it is Asked,	131
VI.	On the "Treachery" of the American Indian,	141

A GLANCE AT CURRENT HISTORY.

A GLANCE AT CURRENT HISTORY.

On the general merits, or rather demerits, of THE SOUTH it is quite evident that the outside world has made up its mind.

The "accepted fable" or "distillation of rumors" which we call history, has fully crystallized, and there seems but little ground for supposing, during the present generation, that there will be any revision of the judgment already pronounced.

For two-and-thirty years our Northern friends have deprecated any allusion on our part to the causes or character of the war, assuring us that every impulse of manhood and every throb of patriotism demanded that we should bury the past, with all its illusive hopes and unavailing griefs, and bend our undivided energies to the upbuilding of a common country. And that is precisely the thing which we have been doing.

Meantime, during those same two and thirty years, those Northern friends of ours have been diligent in a systematic distortion of the leading facts of American history—inventing, suppressing, perverting, without scruple or shame—until our Southland stands to-day pilloried to the scorn of all the world and bearing on her front the brand of every infamy.

This has been accomplished not alone nor chiefly by historic narrative or formal record, but rather by the persistent use, at all times and on all occasions, of every form and mode of unfriendly expression—in pulpit and on platform, at lyceum and on the hustings, by picture and story, by

A GLANCE AT CURRENT HISTORY. 13

essay and song, by sedate disquisition and airy romance, and in a general way by the unwearied false coloring of all past and current events.

Step by step the malignant work has gone on. Each point yielded by Confederate silence has been swiftly seized as a new vantage ground for Federal aggression. The forbearance of the South has been misconstrued. In her solicitude for the honor of the American name, she has refrained from either vindicating herself or characterizing the conduct of her conquerors. Like the true mother at the judgment seat of the Great King she has accepted injustice rather than bring under condemnation the child of her own being.* And she has her reward.

For thus it has come to pass that in the popular mind her very name has been made

---

*The domain of Virginia originally extended from Carolina to Canada, and from the Atlantic ocean to the Pacific.

an embodiment of folly, a symbol of meanness, a proverb of utter and incurable inefficiency. The economist with a principle to illustrate, the moralist full of his Nemesian philosophy, the dramatist in quest of poetic justice—in short every craftsman of tongue or pen with a moral to point or a tale to adorn turns instinctively to this mythical, this fiction-created South, and finds the thing he seeks.

The world has decided against us, and there remains to us now but a single hope—the hope of winning and holding something better than a dishonored place in the hearts of our own children. And even this hope, modest yet none the less precious, is fading away as the days go by. A wise and philosophical historian has justly said that "a people which takes no pride in the noble achievements of a remote ancestry will never achieve anything worthy to be remembered by remote descendants." Truer words were never spoken. And yet our grandchildren, trained in the public schools, often mingle with their affection an indefinable pity, a pathetic sorrow—solacing us with their caresses while vainly striving to forget "our crimes." A bright little girl climbs into the old veteran's lap, and hugging him hard and kissing his gray hairs, exclaims: "I don't care, grandpa, if you were an old rebel! I love you! I love you!"

But there is to be an end of this. The friends of the Grand Army of the Republic have spoken. And ever since the war ended, that army has been a potential force. Nothing more is to be said in palliation of the rebels or the rebellion—no word of comfort, no plea of sympathy. Confederates are always to be described as "insurrectionists" who sought to destroy the Government. "Treason is to be made odious." The story of the war is to be told from the victor's standpoint alone. The existing histories are to be expurgated. Every tribute to Southern heroism is to be blotted out, and the sum total of martial glory is to be transferred to the Grand Army of the Republic.

This plan has doubtless many advantages. It seems to settle hard questions so easily. Military fame is illusive, and if it comes not by gage of battle, there is really nothing more natural than to invoke it by other means. And our Northern friends have chosen wisely. If the three tailors of Tooley street could achieve undying renown by putting forth a mere preamble, what may not the friends of the Grand Army accomplish by writing down a solid column of resolutions? They have labored long and arduously, but have at last hit the mark. We admire their perseverance, their resourcefulness, but most of all we felicitate them on their success in giving a new meaning to the old aphorism that "the pen is mightier than the sword."

The United States History which to day enjoys the widest circulation and the highest fame is the recent work of GOLDWIN SMITH, Doctor of Canon Law and Professor of the Humanities, Toronto, Canada.

The learned author has gathered his inspiration, and what he calls his facts, from many sources. He enumerates by title no less than twenty-two authorities, and adds that a complete list would be out of proportion to the size of the book itself. And yet there is absolutely nothing to indicate that he has troubled himself with more than one side of his subject. He makes no allusion of any kind to any writer who has extended his investigations in the faintest degree beyond the beaten paths of Northern historical orthodoxy. There is not a fragment of reference to Sage's colossal work, or the scholarly monograph of Curry, or the vivid picturings of Maury, or the comprehensive exposition of Stephens, or the philosophical review of Ropes, or indeed any citation whatever which can inspire a reasonable hope of the slightest tendency towards impartial treatment.

Mr. Goldwin Smith, however, is something more than a mere Doctor of Canon Law and Professor of the Humanities. He takes high rank among the masters of political economy, and surely not without abundant reason, for the skill with which he has adapted his wares to his market is beyond all praise.

His book is published both at New York and London, and is intended, he informs us, "for English rather than American readers;" nevertheless, it has become amazingly popular with our brethren throughout the North.

The general plan of his work is an unsparing villification of the South. This wins for him Northern plaudits. Amid the gleeful tumult he weaves in his sneers and

A GLANCE AT CURRENT HISTORY. 19

gibes on America at large, and thus opens a second market for his books among his own class of delighted Britishers.

South Carolina, he says, got her start by combining "buccaneering with slave owning," and utilized her ports by making them a shelter for pirates and corsairs, "such as Captain Kidd and Blackbeard."

Georgia he deals with more leniently. Her people were not distinctly criminal, but just languidly and lazily vicious—shiftless, drunken and beggarly. She became "the refuge of the pauper and the bankrupt." Her first settlers were "good-for-nothings who had failed in trade"—a "shiftless and lazy set," who "called for rum;" but later on "better elements came in, Highlanders, Moravians, and some of the persecuted Protestants of Salzburg."

But Virginia seems to be his especial aversion. From her very beginning it has been her misfortune to awaken within him the most distressing emotions. He says she was not started right; that her first settlers were an unpromising lot—lackeys, beggars, broken-down gentlemen, tapsters out of a job. And things went from bad to worse. "To the crew of vagabonds were afterwards added jail-birds." * * "Convicts were offered their choice between the gallows and Virginia," and some were wise enough to choose the gallows. They were not nice. Their aims were low, their motives sordid, "their very place of settlement has long been a desolation, and only fragments of ruin mark its site."

Such is the forbidding background of Mr. Goldwin Smith's historical picture when he begins to light it up with the luminous glories of the Plymouth settlement. The Pilgrims, he assures us, were an altogether different kind of people. There was nothing sordid about them, nothing grovelling, nothing base. Their pure hearts were too full of simple faith and holy zeal to afford room for corrupting influences or worldly desires. "Some sustaining motive higher than gain was necessary to give them victory in their death struggle with nature, to enable them to make a new home for themselves in the wilderness, and to found a nation."

It was not only during the early period of colonization that the New Englanders were superior to the Virginians. The distinction seems to have widened as time went on. "Though no longer gold seekers, the men of Virginia were not such colonists as the Puritans. They were more akin in character to the Spaniard on the south of them, who made the Indian work for him, than to the New Englander, who worked for himself." * * "To work for them they had from the first a number of indentured servants, or bondsmen, jail-birds, many of them; some kidnapped by press gangs in the streets of London, all of depraved character." * * "Afterwards came in ever-increasing volume African slavery, the destined bane of Virginia and her ultimate ruin. Thus were formed the three main orders of Virginia society: the planter oligarchy, the 'mean white trash,' and the negro slaves." And so for two hundred years she plodded on, unredeemed, her "poor whites" being hopelessly given over to "a barbarous and debased existence."

As were the people so were their leaders. "A chief fomenter of the quarrel" [with England] "was Patrick Henry, a man who had tried many ways of earning a livelihood, and had failed in all." * * * "A brankrupt at twenty-three, he lounged in thriftless idleness, till he found that tho he could not live by industry he could live by his eloquent tongue."

This is the Goldwin Smith idea incarnate. It is the Yankee idea, the Puritan idea.

The logical New England brain would formulate and demonstrate the proposition thus:

1. Patrick Henry, furnished with a good stock of groceries, failed at twenty-three.

2. A Puritan, even of the tenth magnitude, under like circumstances, would not fail at twenty-three.

Ergo: A tenth-rate Puritan is the superior of Patrick Henry.

Such are the limitations of the New England mind. Under the law of its very being it is fettered by its single standard of worth, and is therefore qualified to pass judgment only on those subjects which by it are measurable or deemed worthy of measurement. Its supreme test of merit is accumulation; the capacity to amass.

As a student of natural history our author has doubtless been taught that the eagle is without a rival in range of vision or strength of wing. And yet he should know that the busy magpie in half an hour will spy out and stow away more bits of glass and shining beads and glittering trumpery of every sort than the Bird of Jove will be likely to get together in a score of years. Mr. Goldwin Smith does not seem to make proper allowance for differences in instinct.

A generous foe, a member of the aristocratic order which Henry so fiercely assailed, sees in the young Virginian something other than a "shiftless idler" and "lounging bankrupt." The poet-peer felicitously presents him to all nations and to all ages as "the forest-born Demosthenes"—the standard-bearer of a brave people, outraged by unendurable wrongs, yet resolute to transmit to their posterity the liberties which were their birthright.

With that prescience which is the heaven-bestowed gift of genius the young patriot clearly discerned the signs of the times. He foresaw the real nature of that tempest which was fast gathering throughout the civilized globe. He knew that tho the world for two centuries had been awakening from its lethargy of a thousand years, yet the time was only then ripening for mankind's deliverance. Instead of minding his shop, as Mr. Goldwin Smith would have done; instead of consecrating himself heart and soul to movements in the tallow trade or fluctuations in the calico market, he gave his brilliant intellect free range through the whole cycle of human knowledge, and summed up the situation of the hour with a precision and comprehensiveness which is still the marvel of statists and historians and political philosophers.

He saw the forces of tyranny marshalling themselves on every hand against the spirit of liberty, and he saw that the spirit of liberty was everywhere the spirit of the age. He foretold the nature of the coming struggle, with its burden of grief for every home in Western Europe. He heard the tread of mighty armies and the sorrowing cry of oppressed multitudes; a cry which was soon to change its accent and precipitate that frightful conflict which shook the earth. The hour was approaching when monarchs and priests and conquerors must unite to try conclusions in a death grapple with the awakened peoples—an hour when the new world might sever the ligatures which bound it to the old—an hour when America by one bold stroke might fling off the ancient traditions which else would forever entrammel her with the abuses and superstitions of a despotic and benighted past.

It was for the work of that hour that Patrick Henry was born.

The informed historian discerns in him, not the "storm petrel of revolution," but the defender of inherited liberties. He came at a moment when free institutions were trembling in the balance. The old theory of kingly right to govern wrong was being again asserted. The illimitable and unchecked right to tax was declared in the very terms which had demanded benevolences and ship-money. Lord North and the Earl of Bute and George the Third had formed a triune despotism which bore every mark of the despotism of Strafford and Laud and Charles the First. And it was the lot of Patrick Henry at that crucial moment to lead the forlorn hope of constitutional liberty just as John Hampden had led it, under the same conditions, a hundred years before.

It is nothing to the purpose that the colonies won their independence, their Statehood, a few years before the coming of the grand catastrophe. Their action was simply the first episode of that mighty drama. The prize battled for was the boon of civil liberty; the people interested were the civilized nations; and it was needful that the first blow should come from the Western hemisphere. And it is the glory of Henry that his genius discerned the end from the beginning—that he saw in the approaching downfall of crown and scepter and mitre, and all the infinite paraphernalia of old world oppression, mankind's best hope for the new world's deliverance. And so amidst the first mutterings of the storm which was to culminate in universal wreckage—amidst the portents which prefigured the vision of tottering thrones and shattered dynasties and crumbling empires, he upheld the brave faith that then and there might be laid, broad and deep, the enduring foundations of the temple of American liberty.

It is safe to say that throughout his entire work Mr. Goldwin Smith never calls the name of a Virginian without bestowing upon him the tribute of his scorn.

If sometimes he seems to praise Washington it is only that he may be the better able to mark, by force of contrast, the worthlessness of his followers and the badness of his cause.

"Without him," says Mr. Goldwin Smith, that cause "would have been ten times lost," and "the names of those who had drawn the country into the conflict would have gone down to posterity linked with defeat and shame." Still, continues the author, "we can hardly number among great captains a general who acted on so small a scale," one who "never won a battle," and whose final success after all "was due not to native valor but to foreign aid." The chief merit which he grants to Washington was "his calmness and self-control in contending with the folly and dishonesty of Congress and the fractiousness of the State militia." As a commentary on the times he quotes a casual remark of Governeur Morris: "'Jay,' ejaculated Governeur Morris thirty years afterwards, 'what a lot of d——d scoundrels we had in that Second Congress!' 'Yes,' said Jay, 'we had,' and he knocked the ashes from his pipe." In a nation where all are blind, a one-eyed man will be king. And such is substantially the distinction which Mr. Goldwin Smith accords to George Washington.

James Madison, one the most eminent and blameless statesmen of any age or nation is curtly dismissed as "a well-meaning man, but morally weak."

Henry Clay, orator, patriot, pacificator—passionately beloved by his friends and honored even by his political opponents—devoted beyond all else to the welfare of his country, and ever ready to make any sacrifice at the shrine of an unbroken Union—who Curtius-like flung himself time and again into the abysses of sectional discord, and whose whole life was a concordance of the placid words he spoke when he met his political defeat, "it is better to be

A GLANCE AT CURRENT HISTORY. 31

right than president;"—this man, able, pure, magnanimous, generous in his ambitions, avowed in his convictions; steadfast in his aims, true to his friends, charitable to his opponents, flexible in expedients yet firm as the primal rocks where principle was involved; this man, the latchet of whose shoes his accuser is not worthy to unloose, is flippantly denounced as a mere "political acrobat," a "dazzling but artful politician who owed his fall to a false step in the practice of his own art."

John Randolph, he tells us, had "natural ability" but lacked "good sense" and had "no power of self-control." * * * "With the arrogance of his class he would enter the Senate with his hunting whip in his hand, and behave as if he were in his kennel."

The "behavior" of Virginians seems indeed to be a subject of ever-recurring solicitude with Mr. Goldwin Smith. For he is exceeding strong on questions of deportment—a weighty judge of "leather and prunello."

> "Let arts and commerce, laws and learning die,
> But, give us back our old nobility!"

He makes the customary fling at "plantation manners," but is mildly surprised that "Franklin and Samuel Adams" should have been "lacking in the ordinary traits of gentlemen." As for Patrick Henry nothing better was to be expected, since "the character of an English gentleman" is not to be formed "on a plantation or in the backwoods,"—an opinion by the way which is anything but English if we exclude such authorities as the distinguished author, the 'Arrys and 'Arriotts of Bow Bells, and the eminently respectable contingent of Servants' Hall.

The only American whom Mr. Goldwin Smith seems to hold in real regard is Gen-

A GLANCE AT CURRENT HISTORY. 33

eral Benedict Arnold. "Arnold," he says, "was one of the best of the American commanders and perhaps the most daring of them all." * * * "He was slighted and wronged by the politicians," and "seems to have despaired of the cause." As a patriot "he shrank from the idea of the French alliance." He believed "that France had designs on Canada." Under those circumstances he resolved to enact the role of General Monk, and to that end opened negotiations with the British Commander.

In his treatment of incident Mr. Goldwin Smith is no less buoyant and free-handed than in his judgment of character. He has no prejudices; no bias. All kinds of knowledge are equally welcome; all sources of information equally meritorious. Any rumor of the camp, any scrap of idle gossip, any stray vagary of the newspaper correspondent, so it meets his needs, is accounted proper pabulum for the Muse of History.

Here are a few of his utterances, taken almost at random:

"Jefferson Davis when captured" was "farcically disguised in woman's clothes."

"The slaveholders escaped military service while they thrust the poor under fire."

"Confederate prisoners were well fed, and suffered no hardships." * * * "If many of them died it was because the caged eagle dies."

"Guards pressed men in the streets" of Southern cities, and "conscripts were seen going to Lee's army in chains."

The Southern clergy were "not only ignorant but cringing and degraded."

"Jackson was nicknamed 'Stonewall'" because of his steadfastness "on a field of general panic."

Wilkes Booth was "a ranting Virginia

A Glance at Current History. 35

actor" who drew his inspiration from "the tyrannicide motto of his State."

"At the taking of Fort Pillow the negroes were nailed to logs and burned alive."

"Copperheads were so called from a reptile which waits on the rattlesnake, the rattlesnake being emblematic of the South."

"The Northern press, unlike the slave press of the South, never misled the people by publishing false news of military successes."

"The Southern lady was but the head of a harem." She "might be soft, elegant, and charming, tho there was an element in her character of a different kind, which civil war disclosed."

Slanders and perversions such as these seem unworthy of serious refutation. They arouse loathing rather than resentment. And so amid our unutterable and unuttered contempt they generally escape rebuke. Yet the world believes them. It is nothing that many of these fables are foolish and incredible in themselves. It is nothing that they are false to nature, false to fact, false to the canons of fiction. It is nothing that they confute each other. It is nothing that they would be mutually destructive if they should meet, for they are scattered throughout many pages and are digested singly.

Frightful stories are told of horrible torture inflicted by Southerners on their hapless prisoners. And charming pastorals are written on the lovingkindness of the Northern people as manifested by their beneficent treatment of the captives in their hands. And yet when Mr. Goldwin Smith is confronted by the official prison records on each side—when it is shown that the death rate in Northern prisons exceeded the death rate in Southern prisons by nearly eight per cent.—the versatile author has his ready reason: "If many of the Southerners died it was because the caged eagle dies."

This in a sense is true, and is a just tho unconscious tribute to the soldiery of the South. Many of them did die as the caged eagle dies; they did beat out their hearts against the prison bars; their spirits at last did sink; their eyes, dauntless in battle, did grow dim. And so, tho they were still unsubdued, their pulses ceased at last to beat, and only their mortal clay remained to those who could destroy their bodies but could not quell their souls.

The fidelity of the Confederate captive is without a parallel in human history. At any hour of any day freedom was his on the simple condition of swearing allegiance to the "Government of the United States."

But what was the mood of this Southern soldier—this scion of a race of freemen—this bold spirit who under duress "dies as the caged eagle dies;" what was his mood of mind while he was being dragged "to Lee's army in chains?" Where then were beak and claw and strength of wing? And with what sort of thrusting instrument did the "shirking slaveowners" "thrust him under fire? And how many chained eagles could one thruster "thrust forward at a time?" Or rather, perhaps, how many "shirking slaveholders" would be required to "thrust under fire" a single eagle, chained or unchained?

And is not the South entitled to some off-set against the North on the score of this special cause of death? Was it only on one side that the vital spark was quenched by loss of liberty? Did no imprisoned Northern soldier "die as the caged eagle dies?" Would each and all have been happy and contented if "well fed" and sheltered from "hardship?" Was it the Southern soldier alone who had none but moral griefs, while the Northern soldier had only material ones? And must indeed these mixed and incongruous absurdities be blindly accepted as rational statements lest the "sacred interests of a broad and generous patriotism" be impaired?

Mr. Goldwin Smith's argument is that the Southern captive, amid boundless abundance, pined and died, yearning for liberty, while the imprisoned Northerner had no thought or care beyond his need of food and shelter, *thus proving* the Southerner to have been of the earth earthy, and the Northerner to have been spiritual in a super-sublimated degree!

It seems a little hard on the unilluminated that they should be expected to digest this sort of reasoning. Yet perhaps we ought to take such logic as we can get, and be thankful for it, inasmuch as the sacred right of might is hard to vindicate unless facts can be forced into harmony with the general hypothesis that the South is a region of savagery while the North is a garden spot of all the christian virtues.

Here are a few more extracts from this "latest and best" of American histories:

"It was a contest," says Mr. Goldwin Smith, "between an iron despotism" on the one hand and "spontaneous zeal" on the other.

"The South," continues the author, "almost from the first, resorted to conscription, ruthlessly enforced by the severest penalties," a course "from which Northern democracy shrank."

"The South," he declares, "had the superiority of force which autocracy lends to war," while "the North had the advantage of the unforced efforts and sacrifices which free patriotism makes."

And as conclusive proof of the invincible strength which "spontaneous zeal" and the "unforced efforts" of "free patriotism" confer upon a "popular government" Mr. Goldwin Smith might aptly have called attention to the memorable interview between the British Minister and the Hon. William H. Seward:

"I can touch a bell at my right hand," said the Secretary of State, "and order the arrest of a citizen of Ohio; I can touch the bell again, and order the arrest of a citizen of New York. Can Queen Victoria do as much?"

Lord Lyons, with closed eyes, slowly and silently shook his head. Yet he might have replied: "It is true, Mr. Secretary, that my sovereign, in this our modern age, has not the authority which you so justly claim; nor indeed had his puissant majesty, George the Third; yet I doubt not that some such proof of power might have been given in the good old days of Henry the Eighth."

The liberty of the press is a subject on which our author grows eloquent—holding that in the North it was absolutely free, while in the South it was but "a sounding board to register the decrees of tyranny." On topics of this class it is really difficult to judge whether or not Mr. Goldwin Smith is writing in good faith. The feeling constantly arises that there is a sly sarcasm, a lurking irony in his praises of the North. In the blandest manner he lays down broad propositions which are not only destitute of truth but which are specifically and in detail the exact reverse of truth.

Every Northern man who lived through the war knows that under the Lincoln government there was no such thing as freedom of the press. It is true that before mobbing or destroying that palladium of liberty the "truly loyal" would lash themselves into a state of moral exaltation by denouncing as "rebel sympathisers" all who dared to remind them of their covenanted obligations—all who dared to quote the Declaration of Independence, or appeal to

A GLANCE AT CURRENT HISTORY. 43

the Constitution of the United States. And so, from the great cities on the Atlantic coast to the little villages on the Western frontier, every opponent of radicalism, every supporter of Statehood, every democratic editor who failed to raise the abject squeak that he was "a war-democrat" was forthwith denounced as an "enemy to free institutions," and patriotically raided, robbed, muzzled and terrorized until crushed out of existence or brought into a loyal frame of mind.

Now turn to the South. During the whole life of the Confederacy her press was absolutely free. Even when confronted by the united hosts of Europe, Asia, and Africa—even when beset by tenfold numbers and by resources mounting up to ten times ten—from the beginning to the end— through all mutations of victory or defeat —no matter what her power or what her needs, the Confederate government, by special enactment, gave absolute exemption from military service to every individual who was connected with her newspaper press.

"A sounding board," indeed! Read the editorials of the chief newspaper published at her capital—the editorials of the RICHMOND EXAMINER. They have been republished in book form since the war and may be easily obtained. The editor was JOHN M. DANIEL—a man of note—able, haughty, resolute; a recluse bitter with the bitterness of misanthropy yet devoured by an insatiable ambition. Passionately pleading for a better equipment in the field, and disgusted with the complacent self-sufficiency of the war office, he assailed the sanctities of that august body, and thence drifted into antagonism with Mr. Davis' entire administration. The breach was never healed, and from the beginning to the end of the war he searched out and gave to open day every blot and every error of every department of the Confederate government. Never since the days of Sir Philip Francis had mortal hand grasped a more trenchant pen, and never was the work of a single pen fraught with more momentous consequences. Under the Lincoln despotism a writer such as Daniel could not have held his liberty a single day.

So much for the "autocracy" which lent the South her "superiority in war." So much for the "iron despotism" which, notwithstanding autocracy, was overthrown by the "spontaneous zeal" of the North!

Does not Mr. Goldwin Smith know that he is giving his readers either pointless sarcasm or utter rubbish? Does he not know that the facts are notoriously and demonstrably the exact reverse of what he states them to be?

Again, the author says that "the South, almost from the first, resorted to conscription, ruthlessly enforced by the severest penalties," a course "from which Northern democracy shrank."

Does he not know that the Northern conscription was as savage and remorseless as that of the invaded country was orderly and mild? Does he not know that what the "spontaneous" patriots really "shrank" from was the decoys and trepanners who filled the union-saving ranks at so much per union-saver? Does he not know that on a single occasion, in the streets of a single Northern city, more than a thousand recusant patriots were shot down like mad dogs while flying in terror before the crimps and kidnappers and press-gangs of the Lincoln government?

But we bid adieu to Mr. Goldwin Smith. He, in turn, is to be set aside. He is altogether too mild a mannered man to meet present demands. His vituperation of the "rebels" falls short in acrimony, while his adulation of the yankees lacks the required unction. ("Rebel" and "Yankee"—how pat as echo the one term calls forth the other.")

The history committee of the Grand Army of the Republic seems to have finally settled on a definite plan. And the plan in some respects is so full of promise that it will doubtless be adopted. The aim is twofold—to render the rebel more odious than history has thus far depicted him, and at the same time to put the yankee in such a position that the world will be compelled to admire him!

For the attainment of so patriotic an end surely nothing more should be needed than the Grand Army's simple requisition. The needful appropriation might be graced by a pæan or two to the old flag, and all should go smoothly. Else, what is the good of victory and victory's lawful fruits?—fame, wealth, honor, reputation, and full control of "history's purchased page?"

The proposed plan is to be official, governmental, authoritative. The required history is to be written by a duly appointed and truly loyal personage who is to gather his war material solely from the "dispatches". on file at Washington. But right there, we apprehend, will be found the fly in the ointment.

Think of it. History by the transcription of yankee dispatches! Bewildering dispatches! Unhappy historian!—the wings of his imagination close clipped, and himself bound by both literary and patriotic obligation to harmonize with the actual situation, and with one another, the varied dispatches of commanders who never, no "never misled the people by publishing false news of military successes!"

Take a handful of the most important dispatches of the war. Or, still better, take the chief dispatches of the Grand Army's chosen heroes—the radical republican generals, the men of immaculate loyalty, the gleaming meteors of war—Benjamin Butler, Banks, Hooker, Pope, O. O. Howard.

Turn to Hooker's dispatch when he had Lee "at his mercy:" "The rebels must attack us in our chosen position, or ingloriously fly!" The rebels did not fly, but they attacked; whereupon the gallant corps of O. O. Howard marched out of history with unexampled alacrity, while the exultant dispatch-bearer spurred hard for Washington with Stonewall's troopers at his heels!

Butler's dispatches are a vibrating note of triumph from Big Bethel in '61 to Bermuda Hundred in '64. The former affair was really a drawn battle, the two wings of his army having lost their way, until they at length collided, whereupon they fired into each other until mutually satisfied, and then simultaneously retired. Butler claimed it as a double victory, but history has not allowed the claim. In his Bermuda campaign he announced his position as being "impregnable against any numbers which the rebels might bring against him." A narrow space between the rivers was the only point of entrance or exit. So Beauregard with a handful of troops turned the position against him, or "bottled him up," as Grant expressed it, and Butler, as a warrior, was heard from no more.

General Banks was pre-eminently distinguished as a dispatch writer, whether waging war amid the cotton bales of the Red River or "chasing the rebels" in the Valley of Virginia. But his campaigns were peculiar, being modeled on the maritime principle of fighting in a circle, so that whenever he overtook the rebels he was pretty sure to find them busy among his supply trains. The hungry Confederates held him in affectionate regard and gener-

A GLANCE AT CURRENT HISTORY. 51

ally spoke of him as "Old Stonewall's Commissary," altho in his dispatches he modestly forbore to mention the rank they gave him.

General Pope was also famous for his dispatches, and never were those dispatches more aglow with victory than whilst he was being cuffed and cudgeled from the banks of the Rappahannock to the walls of Washington. At the very moment that he was declaring the rebels to be in headlong flight, the General-in-Chief, Halleck, frantic with terror, was imploring McClellan to force his marches and save the Capital!

Truly, this official history will be worth the waiting for; particularly as the historian is to be put under orders to arrange the dispatches "patriotically,"—that is, in such shape as to debase the rebel and exalt the yankee!

And yet this subject has its sad side too. The "History" will have its vogue, everybody will want to read it, but during that lively period what will the poor comic papers do?

Those friends of the Grand Army who have a sense of humor are apprehensive that that patriotic body is in danger of being laughed out of existence. And in this emergency it is proposed to enlarge the powers of Government so that a new code of laws may be enacted—laws which shall make it a penal offence to speak with levity of patriotic persons, or to utter reproachful or slighting or irreverent words when speaking of any project which enjoys the support of "loyal" men. A "truthful history" is to be ordered "by act of Congress," and "publishers are to be fined and imprisoned" if they "issue works" which are calculated "to wrongly impress the minds of the growing generation regarding the Rebellion."

Considered as an emanation of the Puritan spirit, all this is perfectly logical. He cares not who fights his battles so that he alone is left to record them. That has always been a Puritan prerogative, and he does not propose to abandon it. He has laid aside his steeple hat and his sour visage and his sad-colored raiment, but at bottom he is the same old Puritan. He has dropped his sanctimonious snuffle and the upward turning of his eyes because he began to perceive that those outward signs of inward grace were putting the unregenerate on their guard against him. But he is still the genuine article. A Pharisee always, he is not to be judged by any common standard; for a being of his lofty pretentions, if not incomparably better than other men, is bound to be immeasurably worse. Moving craftily to his ends, now with a flash of simulated zeal and anon with a placid saintliness, but always disguising his tyranny and greed by special claims to holiness, he is tó-day the same intrusive meddler, with the same inborn passion for regulating other peoples' affairs, that he was when England vomited him forth to the Continent and when the Continent in turn spewed him to the shores of the New World.

Self-styled as the apostle of liberty, he has ever claimed for himself the liberty of persecuting all who presumed to differ with him. Self-appointed as the champion of unity and harmony, he has carried discord into every land that his foot has smitten. Exalting himself as the defender of freedom of thought, his favorite practice has been to muzzle the press and to adjourn legislatures with the sword. Vaunting himself as the only true disciple of the living God, he has done more to bring sacred things into disrepute than has been accomplished by all the apostates of all the ages, from Judas Iscariot to Robert G. Ingersoll.

A GLANCE AT CURRENT HISTORY. 55

Born in revolt against law and order—breeding schism in the Church and faction in the State—seceding from every organization to which he had pledged fidelity—nullifying all law, human and divine, which lacked the seal of his approval—evermore setting up what he calls his conscience against the most august of constituted authorities and the most sacred of covenanted obligations, he yet has the impregnable conceit to pose himself in the world's eye as the only surviving specimen of political or moral worth.

On two occasions he has been clothed, for a brief period, with absolute power, and in each instance he taught his victims what "persecution" really meant. In the tide of time, men have been governed in many ways—by councils and oligarchies—by prophets, priests and kings—by the despotism of tyrants and the despotism of mobs—by fools and philosophers—by learned sages and by savage chieftains—but they knew not the meaning of tyranny until they fell under the Puritan dominion, and learned what it was to be governed by a brood of world-regenerating saints and vanity-inspired busybodies.

"Be you a witch?" roared the embodied majesty of Massachusetts to a trembling paralytic.

"No, your honor," was the reply.

"Officer, said the Court, "take her away and pull out her toe-nails with a pair of hot pincers, and then see what she says; for verily it is written that 'thou shalt not suffer a witch to live!'"

Thus with the act of cruelty goes ever the perverted text.

"We were an hungered, and the salvages had much store of corn, and many garments made of the skins of beasts, and it came to pass that we went forth and fell upon them, smiting them hip and thigh, even with the knife of Ehud and the hammer of Jael, crying aloud and sparing not, and their spoil became an heritage unto us, even unto us and our children."

This precious screed, which serves its turn in sanctifying robbery and murder, is in fair accord with that practical and profitable tenet which has so often been to him a rule of action: "Thou hast said in Thy Word that 'unto the saints should be given the earth and the fulness thereof,' and verily we are the saints."

That the press should be silenced at his bidding, that courts should be reconstructed and constitutions tossed aside, is simply a necessity of the situation. The men of Belial must be put down.

Under ordinary circumstances there should seem to be no particular harm in men's speaking of facts which they had witnessed, or in describing events in which they had participated, or in recording the history which they had made.

But the Puritan has always been a law unto himself, and by virtue of his "superior toleration" he has now become a law unto others. Moreover being guided by that inner light which shines for him alone, there must be no appeal from the justice of his judgments or the righteousness of his decrees.

The Puritan heretofore has made some little amends by furnishing to mankind an enduring target for scorn and mirth and derision. But now we are to be deprived of even that slight compensation—the poor privilege of laughing at him. It is too bad!

It is related of the Roman tyrant, Aurelius Commodus, that, fired by martial ardor, "he entered the arena, sword in hand, against a wretched gladiator who was armed only with a foil of lead, and that after shedding the blood of his helpless victim, he struck medals to commemorate the inglorious victory."

A GLANCE AT CURRENT HISTORY. 59

That fame at any price was precious in the sight of Aurelius is sufficiently evident, yet we nowhere read that he forbade his people to laugh or weep or jibe at his novel way of attaining it.

On the general subject of State Sovereignty, and its relation to secession and nullification, it is well enough to set down a few facts which the coming history will doubtless fail to remember. And if the facts seem "calculated to impress wrongly the minds of the growing generation" why "so much the worse for the facts."

That sterling patriot and life-long Unionist, John Janney, of Loudoun county, was chosen President of the Peace Convention of 1861. On being twitted by a youthful delegate for his State Sovereignty tendencies, the old patriarch said: "Disunion would be the greatest calamity that could befall our State; but, sir, secession is her lawful right, and she alone must determine the expediency of exercising it." * * * "Virginia, sir, is to-day a free and sovereign State; and she was a nation one hundred and eighty years before the Union was born."

This principle of Statehood had been everywhere recognized by Americans up to the time of the war, and nowhere more persistently than by the people of Massachusetts and the New England States.

In her convention of 1780 Massachusetts declared that her people had the sole and exclusive right of governing themselves as a free, sovereign, and independent State, and that they, and they alone, had the indefeasible right to institute, reform, alter or totally change that government whenever their happiness or welfare might seem to require it.

Thirteen years later, when war with Great Britain seemed almost unavoidable, the New

Englanders put forth Hon. Timothy Dwight as their spokesman, and through him declared that they would have no part or lot in such a war, and sooner than have it forced upon them they would go out of the Union.

So, too, when the Louisiana purchase was under discussion. Massachusetts bitterly opposed it and threatened to exercise what she called her "unquestioned right of secession" if the measure should be persisted in. Senator George Cabot was the leader on that occasion.

Indeed, from the very beginning, the New England States left nothing untried to prevent the territorial growth of our country. In the words of Bancroft, "An ineradicable dread of the coming power of the Southwest lurked in New England, especially in Massachusetts." And if they could have had their way, the Mississippi river would now be our western frontier.

Another distinguished secessionist was Senator Pickering, also of Massachusetts. He did not like Mr. Jefferson's administration at all. There was something about it which he said was "not congenial" to his feelings or the feelings of New England. So he proposed a general dissolution of the Union with a view to the formation of a Northern Confederacy. The scheme was favored by New Hampshire, Massachusetts, New Jersey, Rhode Island, Connecticut and Vermont, yet it was deemed imprudent to act without the alliance of New York, who was promised a dominant influence in the new league. But New York declined with thanks and the project fell through.

In 1804 the Legislature of Massachusetts asserted and defined the principle of secession by the following enactment: "That the annexation of Louisiana to the Union transcends the constitutional power of the Government of the United States. It forms a new Confederacy, to which the States united by the former compact are not bound to adhere."

In the debate on the bill for the admission of Louisiana, the representative of Massachusetts, Hon. Josiah Quincy, said: "If the bill passes, it is my deliberate judgment that it is virtually a dissolution of the Union; that it will free the States from their moral obligation; and, as it will be the right of all, so it will be the duty of some, definitely to prepare for a separation—amicably if they can, violently if they must." At this conjuncture a Southern member raised the point that "the suggestion of a dissolution of the Union was out of order; but, on appeal, the House sustained Mr. Quincy, who, in an elaborate argument, vindicated the rightfulness of secession, saying, among other things: "Is there a principle of public law better settled or more conformable to the plainest suggestions of reason than that the violation of a contract by one of the parties may be considered as exempting the other from its obligations? Suppose in private life thirteen form a partnership, and ten of them undertake to admit a new partner without the concurrence of the other three, would it not be at their option to abandon the partnership, after so palpable an infringement of their rights?"

This reasoning goes to the heart of the matter. It asserts that the States are independent political organisms—or rather that they were so in those anti-bellum days—and that all the massed power of majorities could not drag down the principle of sovereignty, altho that principle might be enthroned in but a single State.

In 1812 Massachusetts and Connecticut refused to allow their militia to be sent beyond their State lines, and on being left to their own devises they quarrelled with the Administration for refusing to pay them for making a local defense on their own account. Meantime the Governor of Massachusetts occupied himself in calling a public fast-day for deploring the war against a nation which had long been the "bulwark of the religion we profess." The good old town of Plymouth, having risen from its knees, presently got into a muscular mood, and having captured one of the Congressman who voted for the war, forthwith gave a free exhibition of their untrammelled liberty by "kicking him through the town."

Finally the Supreme Court of Massachusetts poured oil on the troubled waters by deciding that neither Congress nor the President had anything to do with the State forces, but that the Governor was the man. So the Governor settled the matter by refusing the request of the President for her quota of troops, and the Massachusetts House of Representatives clinched the whole subject by declaring the war to be unholy, and begging the people to do what they could to thwart it.

In short, on all occasions of domestic disquiet or foreign war the history of New England has been a history of revolt, and threatened separation, and nullification, and secession, and persistent defiance of the authority of Congress and the Federal Courts.

Jefferson's Embargo was never really tried, because the New England States threatened to secede if its provisions should be carried out, and it was accordingly repealed in the vain hope of appeasing them.

But it was on the actual breaking out of hostilities that New England showed the real quality of her "devotion to the Union." She not only did her best to nullify every law passed by Congress for raising men and money, but some of "her best citizens" intrigued with British agents for an alliance with Canada, while others hung out signal lights to enable the enemy's fleet to capture our disabled cruisers—deeds which would have richly deserved the halter if committed by ordinary mortals, but which won for them the enthusiastic plaudits of their kind.

That the Hartford Convention of 1814 was not simply a secession but a treasonable body admits of no rational doubt. The object was not merely to destroy the Union, but to enleague the revolted States with Great Britain, so that the new Confederacy and its ally might be in a position to subjugate the adhering States. The present race of New England apologists pretend that the Convention was "merely an assemblage of some of the Federal leaders," but the plain facts of history discredit their claim. The delegates from Connecticut, Rhode Island and Massachusetts were regularly elected by the Legislatures of those States, and constituted in every respect an official body acting in a representative capacity. Their deliberations were held in secret, and no full account of their proceedings has ever been published, but they publicly announced their adherence to the doctrine of State Sovereignty, full and absolute, declaring that: "When emergencies occur which are either beyond the reach of judicial tribunals or too pressing to admit of delay incident to their forms, States which have no common umpire must be their own judges and execute their own decisions."

In 1861 the Southern people, weary of discord, exercised this sovereign right. They withdrew from their restless and contentious neighbors, and formed a more harmonious Union among themselves, asking only to be let alone. The "emergency" which confronted them was the enthronement of a hostile and revolutionary faction—a faction which at a fatal moment had come into power through a triple division among the law-abiding classes.

These new rulers had chiefly distinguished themselves as the enemies of existing institutions—their political and social creed being, in effect, "Whatever is, is wrong." They were fond of execrating the Union as "a league with hell," and denouncing the Constitution as "a covenant with death." They derided the highest courts of the land as "crimping houses of iniquity," and villified the old flag as "a flaunting lie!"

But on coming into power they threw off all disguise, and shamelessly started a war of conquest in pretended defense of the very principles and symbols which they had so bitterly reviled.

With paralyzing logic they mutilated the States on the plea that the States were "indestructible;" they debarred them from the Union while declaring the Union to be "indissoluble," and they patched up and distorted the Constitution on the pretence that they were the only class who reverenced its "inviolability." Having thus approved themselves the only true champions of "the sacred principle of government by consent," they rounded out their perfect work by converting the States into satrapies, and holding them under bayonet rule until the conquered people consented to ratify the whole of their rump performances. No wonder they are yearning for a historian of their own!—no wonder they are drafting laws to give that historian sole control of the facts!

As for the South, she accepted war when no other recourse was left her. And she has borne its results, bitter tho they have been, with the serenity of fortitude and the dignity of silence. Conscious of rectitude in aim and deed, she has been willing to leave her cause to the tribunal of posterity. Like the princess in the Eastern story, she has held her course, unshaken by clamor, unmoved by taunts and sneers, and without one backward glance has swept on toward the Golden Fountain of the Future. She has been content to leave her name and memory "to men's charitable speeches, to foreign nations and the next age." She frankly concedes that under the new Union, and the revised Constitution, and the improved laws, and the generally amended polity, there may have been innovations with which she has not kept pace, and which she does not fully comprehend. But when she is threatened with pains and penalties for presuming to relate to her own children the simple annals of her life, she believes that it is fairly within her right to enter a mild and respectful yet earnest protest.

*

ON HISTORY AS TAUGHT IN OUR SCHOOLS.

A LETTER OF INVITATION.

The following circular letter explains itself. It was heartily responded to, and resulted in a magnificent assemblage at Lee Camp Hall on the evening of October 19, 1897. The meeting was addressed by a number of the foremost citizens of Virginia, among them: Consul-General Fitzhugh Lee, Governor O'Ferrall, Mayor Taylor, Dr. Hunter McGuire, Colonel Gordon McCabe, Professor McGuire, and others. A permanent organization was effected, with Dr. McGuire as presiding officer, and the proposed task of banishing false histories from the schools and colleges of the State was promptly entered upon and seems in a fair way of being thoroughly accomplished.

ON HISTORY AS TAUGHT IN OUR SCHOOLS.

Headquarters Grand Camp Confederate Veterans, Department of Virginia, Glen Allen, Va., September 29, 1897.

DEAR SIR,—The Grand Commander, as authorized by the Advisory Council, hereby extends to you a cordial invitation to attend a general meeting to be held at Lee Camp Hall, in Richmond, Va., on Tuesday, October 19, 1897, at 8 o'clock P. M.

This proposed gathering of leading educators and eminent citizens of Virginia is called for the purpose of formulating a definite plan for the exclusion from our schools and colleges of all histories which are grossly erroneous in their statements, or which, in their animus, are unfriendly to the State.

A careful examination of those school histories which are now in general use among us discloses the fact that they are all written by persons who placidly assume that the American States in some unexplained way had divested themselves of their Statehood at some unnamed period prior to 1860, and that the States which at that time exercised their sovereign right by withdrawing from the federal union thereby committed an act of "rebellion" against their former associates!

This false assumption, first urged by desperate partisans, and afterwards dogmatised into an article of faith, now dominates all these Northern historians, and vitiates every portion of their work. And thus our ingenuous youth are taught to believe that their fathers were traitors to their country and subvertors of the Constitution and the laws. True, in most of these histories the word "rebel" has been cancelled, and in its place the term "confederate" now appears; and there are also favorable comments on the prowess of these confederates and on the military skill of their leaders. But always and everywhere the inference is constant that the Southern people were false to the obligation of patriotism and enemies of their country.

Lord Macaulay utters an important truth when he declares that "a people who take no pride in the achievements of their ancestors will never achieve anything worthy to be remembered by their descendants." And our conquerors now assure us that the highest favor we can expect from the world is "its merciful silence."

Are we indeed reduced to this narrow choice between infamy and oblivion?

Let us hope not.

And let us act on that hope.

There is no desire to re-open settled questions, or to evade the physical results of the war. We accepted an appeal to the sword, and we abide the result without repining. But never did we put to the hazard of war our right to speak the truth, or the right of our children to hear it.

Our race, from the dawn of its history, has freely criticised the acts and views and purposes of both friend and foe. Briton and Dane, Saxon and Norman, Yorkist and Lancastrian, Puritan and Cavalier, in song and story and on the written page have recounted their stirring deeds through a thousand years; and ever the defeated side, strengthened by adversity and nourished by tales of fortitude, has risen again to the level of its victor; and the conflicting breeds, welded not less by war than by comity, have become at last the master-race of all the earth. Their stories of mutual strife awaken a spirit of generous emulation, and the memorials of their fellest battles adorn a common Pantheon and augment their heritage of a common glory. For in an atmosphere of free utterance, hatred cannot long abide. It is born of a sense of injustice, and gathers its chief nourishment from repression. And so, in behalf of a rational and lasting concord—a concord open as the day—with nothing to conceal and nothing to simulate—standing on exact level with our conquerors—we propose to follow the ancient usage of our race. We propose to relate the annals of our own war to our own children in our own way. We propose to describe in the plainest and simplest language the causes and the character of that war. For only thus can we rescue from infamy the memory of our fallen comrades. Only thus can we pay a fitting tribute to the devotion of our noble women. Only thus can we blot out the felon-brand of "TRAITOR" from the kingly brow of Robert Edward Lee.

Let not our Northern friends mistake our purpose. The war is over. Decisive battles are the expression of a law which is beyond themselves; they follow the trend of events and are but the incidents of a power which overshadows them. Appomattox was the culmination of a strife which was active before the Union was born, and the decree there rendered is as absolute and as irrevocable as that of Culloden or of Hastings. Never again will peril approach our country on territorial lines. What may arise within the heart and centre of the Republic it were idle to conjecture. Perhaps only a phantom, formless and void. But should that phantom take shape, should it cast its dark shadow along the northern horizon, it might well befall that the despised South, true to herself, unshaken in her integrity, faithful to her traditions and her principles, might again lead in giving to all our land the priceless boon of freedom joined with order, of liberty linked with law.

If, sir, you share the views thus meagerly outlined, or any of them, it is earnestly hoped that you will join us in this effort. We need your counsel, your influence, your intellectual and moral support. The eleventh hour is upon us, and unless we act unitedly and with sustained energy the memory of our Cause will go down to posterity loaded with derision and shame.

We sincerely hope that you will come, at almost any sacrifice, to help in this patriotic work.

By order of

JOHN CUSSONS,
THOMAS ELLETT, *Grand Commander*.
Adjutant-General.

ON "TEACHABLE" HISTORY.

GRAND COMMANDER'S ADDRESS.

The object of the Lee Camp Hall Meeting of September 29, 1897, was outlined by the Grand Commander in the following address:

ON "TEACHABLE" HISTORY.

* * * * * *

The hearty applause that greeted Dr. McGuire's utterances had hardly died away when Colonel Cussons came forward. He was given a most cordial greeting, which he acknowledged with a bow. The Grand Commander spoke in clear voice and with great vigor and earnestness. He said:

Mr. Chairman, Friends, Comrades,
Ladies and Gentlemen:

Seven years ago the Confederate Veterans of Virginia, through their Grand Camp, appointed a committee on history. The chief object was to point out the need for a textbook which should give a fair and impartial account of our late war. And it was believed that the appearance of such a work would at once banish from our schools the biassed and misleading histories which were then in use. That hope has been disappointed. It is true that able pens responded promptly to the committee's call, and Virginia to-day is notably rich in school histories of the very highest order. And yet these meritorious books have failed to displace the unworthy ones.

In literary ability, in fidelity to truth, in lucidity of narrative, in simplicity of style, in skill of compression, and in all the mechanical qualities which comprise the bookmaker's art, we shall nowhere find anything superior to the works of our own Virginia writers. And these books have the widest range of adaptability. They are suited to pupils of every age. From Mrs. Williamson's "Life of Lee," a model of

historical biography for the infant class—
through the primary and advanced text-
books of Maury and Dr. Jones, and Mrs.
Pendleton Lee, and Miss Mary Tucker
Magill—up to the sedate and scholarly exposition of J. L. M. Curry, there is absolutely no need which has not been most
abundantly met.

What, then, bars the way? Why is it
that we cannot get into the hands of our
own children these annals of our own life
by our own authors?

I hold in my hand a symbol of the
power which forbids it.

This history, among all the histories
which have been written in this historic
age, is the only one, we are gravely informed, that is at all adapted to school-room
requirements—the only one which possesses
the mystic attribute of "*teachability!*"

And, surely, if "*teachability*" means an
aptitude for reaching false conclusions by

smooth and subtle ways—for making the worse appear the better part—for blandly distorting facts, and with an air of candor preverting honest truths—then, indeed, may this book be pronounced "*teachable*" in a very eminent degree.

Like some other evil things, it is sugared over with adulation. And where it most abounds in florid compliment it is most misleading and most dangerous. Its worst vices, however, are not of the gross and obvious kind. They are unobtrusive. They lie beneath the surface. But they are constant; and during the war period they are close-woven into the very texture of the story. To adequately show this by citations would be a tedious task. And to quote a passage here and there would be to imitate the traveller who tried to give his friends an idea of the magnitude of the Coliseum by showing them a few bricks which he had wrenched out of its walls.

On "Teachable" History. 93

Here is a specimen brick: "Invasion of Maryland." This book always calls it an "invasion" when Southern troops go North. When Northern troops go South it calls it "marching to the front." I quote: "Flushed with success, Lee now crossed the Potomac and entered Maryland, hoping to secure volunteers and excite an insurrection."

Think of it. Robert E. Lee an insurrectionist!

That is what we have been teaching our children for years. That is what we are teaching them to-day. Is it any wonder that they are getting a bit ashamed of us? that they are telling us "the less said about the war the better?"

But while we are on the subject of insurrection, let us see what this *teachable* history has to say about Old Ossawattomie Brown, the Free-Soil desperado of Kansas. Brown was reputed the most lawless and the most fearless of all those freebooters—a man of iron nerve and bloody hand—and with this reputation he was chosen by the New England Abolitionists to carry fire and sword to the peaceful homes of Virginia. It was those social regenerators who furnished forth his military chest. They equipped him with weapons for the arming of a thousand men, and sent him on a crusade which must inevitably seal his doom unless he should be able to incite and maintain that most frightful of all human scourges—a servile insurrection!

And what does this *teachable* history have to say about it?—this history which teaches that Lee was an insurrectionist? We find Brown exalted into a hero and a martyr, rather than a criminal. He is depicted as a brooding enthusiast, inspired by lofty motives, but unable to carry out his great designs.

No hint is given of the men whom he cruelly murdered on that tranquil Sabbath morning at Harper's Ferry. No mention is made of the peaceful citizens whom he seized in their beds, and shackeled as hostages, or slew from mere lust of blood. In short, we are assured that these deeds of his had really no meaning in them. And if any one was to blame it was the Southern people, who, this *teachable* history tells us, put themselves in a wrong light by getting excited and rushing to the conclusion that the raid was "significant of Northern sentiment." "It was soon known," says this history, "that in his wild design Brown had asked counsel of no one," and with this cool prevarication the whole subject is dismissed. There is no allusion to the tolling of funeral bells on the day of his execution. There is no mention of special services at churches draped in mourning, or of flags hanging at half-mast. And yet these things were so. And to-day he stands in apotheosis, the divinity of a new sect, with an aureole about his brow, and a legend which declares that his mode of death "has made the gallows as sacred as the cross." And his name and fame have united to inspire, if not our national anthem, at least the battle-song of the republic's conquering armies.

The instincts of the South were right! In the incursion of this tough old marauder, half highwayman, and half fanatic, we had premonition of other hordes, more numerous, yet not more scrupulous, who, like him, were to ravage the land with a zeal quickened by rapacity, with a rapacity sanctified by zeal.

I should like to call your attention to the cold and formal terms which are used in relating Federal disasters, and to contrast them with the effusion and glow and tumult which depict their victories. The Army of the Potomac, this *teachable* history informs us, was "checked" at Fredericksburg; and again "checked" at Chancellorsville. Which is very true! It is likewise true that the army of Bonaparte was "checked" at Waterloo. But no French patriot, not even Victor Hugo, ever thought of putting it in that way!

Now, turn the page, and see a Federal victory. We are carried at once into a new atmosphere—an atmosphere of the vivid, the picturesque, the dramatic. Behold Sheridan—the illustrious, and the illustrated—he of the "coal-black steed," spurning the dull earth beneath him, "covered with foam," his nostrils blown wide open, his tail in convulsions, "dashing to the new front," and sending the "plundering Confederates whirling up the Valley of the Shenandoah."

On the next page in a foot-note, there is a brief reference to one of *our* cavalry commanders, General Forrest. It is the only mention that this *teachable* history makes of that remarkable man, and every word is to his disparagement. And yet in all quarters of the globe, wherever the art of war is studied, the career of Forrest has been a marvel and a delight. A wandering star in the military firmament, his magnitude has not yet been measured nor his orbit traced, but his dazzling coruscations have bewildered the strategists of all climes and tribes, from Delhi to Kamschatka, from Sierra Leone to the Horse Guards. What would have been disaster and black ruin to other commanders was to him but a mild exhilaration. Hemmed in by tenfold numbers, we catch again the inspiration of his cheery words:

"Now, men; we've got 'em just right! They're all around us, and whichever way we go we shall mix up with 'em!"

Truly, it might be said of him:

"Most master of himself and least encumbered
When most beset, surrounded and outnumbered."

At First Manassas (Bull Run) we have the astounding information that "the Confederates were driven from the field," but were subsequently rallied. Then a shell burst among the teamsters' wagons, a caisson was upset, and McDowell's men fled, etc. This trick of statement runs all through the book. It is never the "Northern army" that is defeated; but "McDowell's men," or Porter's corps, or the troops under Buell. McDowell, it is true, was one of the nine generals who, in succession, commanded the Army of the Potomac, but we have no right to assume that all school children are familiar with that fact.

The author is definite enough when he describes the battle of Nashville. He does not say that the army of General Hood was "checked." But he says that General Thomas "drove the Confederate forces out of their intrenchments into headlong flight;" that "the Union cavalry thundered upon their heels with remorseless energy," and that "the entire Confederate army was dissolved into a rabble of demoralized fugitives," only "the rear-guard" offering any effective resistance. But he does not tell you that that dauntless rear-guard, which baffled and demoralized and outfought ten times its own numbers, was commanded by the peerless Forrest.

On the fatal third day of Gettysburg this author is equally definite. He does not simply say that Lee's army was "checked," but he goes into details. He depicts it in all the glory of its strength, so that he may show how magnificently his friends destroyed it. "Out of the woods swept the Confederate double battle-line over a mile long." * * * "A thrill of admiration ran along the Union ranks, as, silently and with disciplined steadiness that magnificent column of eighteen thousand men moved up the slope." And then we are told how, when it met its masters, "whole companies rushed as prisoners into the Union lines, while the rest fled, panic-stricken, from the field." Which is not true.

From the summit of Round Top, a prisoner, I saw that charge. I saw groups of Pickett's heroes waving their battle flags and cheering on the crest of the works which they had won. But their ranks had been thinned almost to a skirmish line while they were sweeping through the open valley, and as they closed on their colors to assail the breastworks, their front presented only a series of scanty fragments. A number of these fragmentary bodies, with a heroism never surpassed, carried the works at their front; but soon they were caught in flank and enveloped by the Federal reserves. These movements were skillfully executed, apparently by company officers, and the Federal success, I think, was mainly due to the coolness and courage of those men on the second line. But at best the victory went by a narrow chance. It did not seem to me that it was exclusively "a thrill of admiration" that was running through the Union ranks. Couriers and staff officers were moving too, and wagon trains were thundering to the east, and a rear-guard was swiftly forming, and all the premonitary symptoms of a sudden retreat were in the air. A colonel of cavalry dashed up to the prisoners and threatened to ride down and sabre and utterly exterminate any rebel who should attempt to escape. The rebels responded with a jubilant "hurrah for the Southern Confederacy," and the indignant colonel reviled them and rode away. There were barely a dozen of them—Captain Tom Christian of General Law's staff, and Frank Price of Hood's, and a few scouts from the Texas brigade. But they felt that it was their battle. The cannonade had been effective, and when

Pickett's steady line moved forward there was no one in the vicinity of Round Top who seemed to doubt that it would sweep everything before it.

The day, alas! went against us. But it is not true that "whole companies rushed as prisoners into the Union lines." It is not true that the remnants of that devoted band "fled panic-stricken from the field." The author has been misinformed. These are fabrications. They are smooth, smiling, deliberate Puritan fabrications, and he who coined them will have his portion in the burning lake, his share in the everlasting bonfire. They are needless fabrications. The battle was a brilliant one; the charge superb; gallantly made and bravely met; and to disparage either side is only to belittle the other. They are also shallow and stupid fabrications. Where was the generalship of Meade that he did not spring forward his victorious lines to annihilate this "panic-stricken" crew? Why did he allow Lee, for ten days, to remain on Northern soil, subsisting his troops, conducting his prisoners, and marching along with his ten miles of wagon-trains?

Of Stonewall's brilliant campaign against the four Federal armies of Milroy and Banks and Shields and Fremont there are but a few meagre lines, which conclude with the statement that "Jackson finally made good his escape, having burned the bridges behind him."

And yet our distinguished chairman, who served on Jackson's staff, and who has travelled widely in Europe, will tell you that some of the foremost soldiers and military students of England have declared to him that this campaign was "the finest example of strategy and tactics of which the world

ON "TEACHABLE" HISTORY. 105

has any record; that in this series of marches and battles there was never a blunder committed by Jackson; that this campaign was superior to either of those made by Napoleon in Italy; that it is taught in European colleges as a model of military skill, and that Von Moltke, the great strategist, declares it to be without a rival in the world's history."

Lee's splendid defence against Grant is belittled in the same unworthy spirit. The great Virginian foresaw and thwarted every device of his antagonist. During the first few weeks of that fearful campaign he inflicted on Grant a loss greater than the numbers of his own army. With a skill and vigilance and devotion unparalleled in human annals he held his constantly-lengthening line until it broke from sheer attenuation before the ever-swelling myriads who assailed it. And yet this superb defence, which would outweigh a score of victories won on equal terms, is derided as a mere blind struggle, in which "the dense forests forbade all strategy."

And now steadily, relentlessly, the bitter conflict draws to its close, and this *teachable* history can scarcely hide its glee. "Food failed them." * * "If they sought a moment's repose they were awakened by the clatter of pursuing cavalry. Lee, like a hunted fox, turned hither and thither," but Sheridan closed in upon him.

Is it thus that future ages will contemplate the closing act of that mighty drama? Will no apter figure be found than that of a vile earth-fox to symbolize this Heaven-born leader of men? The comparison comes natural enough to this author, and it harmonizes with the animus of all his work. The "Secessionist," the "plunderer," the "invader," the "insurrectionist," is driven to earth at last, and the writer cannot suppress an inward chuckle.

Shame on those who write such books; and triple shame on those who foist them upon their innocent children! It may be that the power is not in us to withstand the trend of the times. And yet we do know that in the coming years, when, in her own high atmosphere, the Muse of History shall depict the central figure of our fallen cause,—it will not be in the similitude of a prowling fox—predatory in life and abject in death—but rather will there arise before us, serene in native majesty, the august and pathetic image of a noble spirit, tried by every extremity of fortune, yet faithful to the end. The image of

"A great man struggling 'mid the storms of fate,
And greatly falling with a falling State."

ON THE OUTWORN THEORY OF GOVERNMENT BY CONSENT.

AN ADDRESS.

On the 11th of March, 1898, the Department of the Solid South presented to the Confederate Museum a portrait of President Jefferson Davis, on which occasion Colonel Cussons made the following presentation address:

ON THE OUTWORN THEORY OF GOVERNMENT BY CONSENT.

* * * * * *

Promptly at the appointed hour Colonel John Cussons entered the room, and Hon. D. C. Richardson introduced the distinguished soldier, who, he said, "on behalf of the Solid-South Room, will present to the Confederate Museum a portrait of Jefferson Davis, President of the Confederate States of America."

COLONEL CUSSONS' ADDRESS.

Colonel Cussons, as soon as the applause subsided, said:

Friends, Comrades, Ladies and Gentlemen:

On the 11th day of March, 1861—thirty-seven years ago to-day—a nation was born. Calmly, unobtrusively, majestically, it came into being by virtue of the unconstrained political association of seven sovereign States which had withdrawn their adhesion from the Federal Union. At that time no publicist of note denied or doubted the absolute right of those sovereign powers to thus exercise their vital function of sovereignty.

On that fateful day I sat on the portico of the State Capitol at Montgomery, and noted the sedate yet earnest faces of that magnificent assemblage of gentlemen who had been delegated by their several States to adopt a Confederate constitution.

There was no bravado there; no spirit of wanton defiance, either in word or act. Their deliberations were marked by a grave and temperate earnestness, by a realizing sense of the momentous occasion which had called them together. They met the demand of the hour with the patient diligence, the steadfast and serene fortitude of their race.

And I said:

If the Lincoln government shall attempt to despoil these people of their inherited right to govern themselves by lawful methods, in their own way, then must there come a conflict which will not cease while the power of resistance remains—a conflict which will either vindicate for ages yet to come the great American principle of a people's God-given right to self-government; or else that principle, wounded in the house of its friends, will become a by-word and a mockery throughout all lands, and to the remotest times.

Four years later, the drift of events had borne me again to the banks of that same river, and I made my lonely camp with a little remnant of Forrest's gallant men. But there remained in all that region no trace of any familiar thing. The nation had perished. Four years of mortal strife, of immortal glory, of unfading renown. Four years of fortune's fickle moods, her smiles and frowns—of hopes and memories, and blinding tears, and sorrows which would not be assuaged. The nation had perished. Her armies, worn and wasted by victories, were reduced to fragments which could no longer form a battle line. Her opulent cities were a waste. The flower of her youth, the glory of her manhood, had passed away; on wind-swept plains and in pathless forests, a little mound of nameless dust their only sepulchre. Every household in mourning—every home in all the land forlorn and desolate.

Yet are those heroes not forgotten, nor shall they be while patriotism is honored among men, or unavailing sacrifice can claim the tribute of a tear.

> "They fell devoted, yet undying;
> Their names the very winds are sighing;
> The lonely column, cold and gray,
> Claims kindred with their sacred clay.
> Their spirits haunt the dusky mountains;
> Their memory sparkles in the fountains;
> The tiniest rill, the mightiest river,
> Rolls mingled with their fame forever."

The history of those eventful days is the history of the illustrious personage whose portrait the Department of the Solid South now presents to the Confederate Museum.

As the chief of a fallen cause, Jefferson Davis must bear for a season that burden which the Fates ordain for those who sink beneath their frown.

It is easy for the time-server to say that our leader should have surrendered when he saw that the trend of events was against us. But we must remember that to his steadfast and heroic soul there was no middle ground between right and wrong. He stood for the liberties of his countrymen—for those rights which men of our race *must have* or perish in the attempt to attain them!

And even if the Invader had asked the terms on which our chief would cease resistance, the spirit of his reply could have been only that which old Cato sent to all-conquering Cæsar:

> "Bid him disband his legions,
> Restore the Commonwealth to liberty;
> Submit his actions to the public censure,
> And stand the judgment of a free-born people."

Jefferson Davis knew, as none else knew, the real nature and magnitude of the crisis which the South had to confront.

He was dealing with a revolutionary faction which was not amenable to the ordinary dictates of reason and of right—a faction which had denounced the Union, and reviled the Constitution, and aspersed the courts, and villified the nation's flag—a faction which mistook its passions for its conscience, and its freakish fancies for abiding principles—a faction which answered the patriotic appeal for Constitution and Union with the revolutionary counter-cry of "The Union as it is, and the Constitution as it *ought* to be"—a faction which no compact could bind, which no obligation could restrain—a faction which stigmatized the Southern States as an incubus and a reproach, and declared that "they could not be kicked out of the Union"—a faction which dedicated itself to the cause of "equal rights," and poured out all the fervor of its soul in the inspiring phrase, "We hav'nt got any niggers, and we don't mean that you shall have any"*—a faction which

---

*Their lineal descendants, except such as have enriched themselves by plunder, are still uttering the same cry, merely substituting the word "dollars" for "negroes."

resisted the plea for peace by savagely declaring that "the Union would be improved by a little blood-letting"—a faction which started its choicest chapter with professions of the loftiest benevolence, and closed it with that nightmare of horrors, the witches' dance of reconstruction—a faction which inaugurated its reign of peace by instituting terrors more terrible than the terrors of war; which overthrew courts and constitutions, and set up military satrapies on the ruins of Sovereign States—a faction which disfranchised every Southerner of established character, and made the ownership of property a crime; which called to the front of civil power a servile race; a race which had had nothing but its brief tutelage of slavery to uplift it from the barbarism in which it had groped since the creation of the world—a faction which united every phase of folly in its theories with every form of atrocity in its practice;

which instilled into the Negro heart the vile doctrine of "miscegenation," and thus planted the seeds of an evil which now overshadows the land—a faction which daffed aside all laws, human or divine, and called for a new Bible and a new God—a faction which had launched against the South the most ferocious and the most fearless of its fanatical freebooters, a man of iron nerve and bloody hand, who became at last their chosen divinity, and whose name and fame united to inspire the battle-song of their marauding armies. No graver crisis ever confronted a liberty-loving and law-abiding people.

Jefferson Davis's European critics hold that he should have availed himself of the tremendous power which autocracy gives to war; that when the Lincoln Government resorted to despotic measures he also should have met force with force. But those critics forget that the South's struggle was solely for constitutional freedom, for civil privileges and social order, for liberty linked with law.

The whole story of the war and its causes has been distorted and perverted and falsely told. Yet at the bar of unbiased history, before the tribunal of impartial posterity, it will become manifest that the vital principle of self-government—the world's ideal, and what was fondly deemed America's realization of that ideal—went down in blood and tears on the stricken field of Appomattox. It was there that Statehood perished. It was there that the last stand was made for the once-sacred principle of "government by free consent."

The present order of things will go on. The nation will gather strength and prestige and immunity, and power to repress and command, but never again will it be the government which the fathers ordained. Popular in its forms doubtless it will long remain, yet in essence it will be imperial—a vast and opulent yet virtually irresponsible oligarchy, uniting Grecian culture and British strength with something perhaps of Roman pomp and more than Persian magnificence.

The old simplicity and the old integrity of the republic have passed away. The ancient temple of our liberties rested on many pillars, and thence derived its safest strength. But those stately pillars—their sovereign virtue gone—have become but as the slime into which they sank; and thence has emerged the nondescript which we now behold—this thing of shreds and patches—this mock of sovereign states—this federation of political nonentities which no two statists in the land can agree upon, or define alike.

Potential classes are now longing for a change; they are earnest in their desire for what they call "a strong government." And it may be that their yearnings will not be in vain. The corruption of a republic is the germination of an empire. A period of domestic turbulence or foreign war would render usurpation as easy as the repetition of a thrice-told tale. Political speculations would then reassume their old names—incivism, sedition, constructive treason—and the familiar remedies would be applied—press censorship, the star chamber, lettres-de-cachet, and bureaus of military justice.

What the gain would be, or what the loss, I do not ask. I merely point to that grand figure, who, through battle-storm and civic tempest, stood staunchly at the helm, and, with the well-worn chart before him, held the prow toward her ancient moorings, as constantly, as unfalteringly, as over midnight billows the needle tracks the polar star.

The ship of state is staunch enough. Her timbers are sound, and her crew is sturdy and brave. But the old chart was shrivelled up by the fierce fires of war, and the old landmarks have been swept away. The wide sea is before us now, and we are drifting; but let us, at least, drift in good hope. The sky is sprinkled thick with gleaming gems, and in the hazard of choosing our beacon let us earnestly pray that we may not follow "all stars of Heaven except the guiding one."

The fame of our dead chief is with the ages and the nations. At a tempestuous period in our history he encountered the fell forces of blind intolerance and fanatic hate, and was crushed beneath their tread. Yet his name and memory will live, and be honored of men, when every memorial of those who overwhelmed him shall have crumbled into indistinguishable dust.

> "For graves like his are pilgrim shrines,
> Shrines to no creed or code confined—
> The Delphic Vales, the Palestines,
> The Meccas of the mind."

Permit me, Governor O'Ferrall, in behalf of the Solid South, to present to the Confederate Museum the portrait of our beloved and honored chief, President Jefferson Davis.

ON GRANTING FORGIVENESS BEFORE IT IS ASKED.

REPLY TO A LETTER

On the subject of inviting the Grand Army of the Republic to become the Guests of the Confederate Capital.

IS IT TO BE DESIRED?

COLONEL CUSSONS ON THE PROPOSED COMING OF THE GRAND ARMY OF THE REPUBLIC.

"The following letter has been received by a gentleman of this city (Richmond, Va.) from Colonel John Cussons, Grand Commander of the Grand Camp of Virginia Confederate Veterans:"

GLEN ALLEN, VA., *August 4, 1897.*
WILLIAM C. PRESTON, ESQ.,
Richmond, Va.:

MY DEAR SIR,—I have read with deep interest your letter of yesterday, and need not say how sedulously we should avoid any act or utterance which might possibly engender friction between the departing and the on-coming generations of our people.

Old Confederates dwell naturally in the past, nursing the memory of the great days which are gone—days rich in promise and in achieved renown—days dark with the gloom of defeat, filled with abiding sorrow, yet never until now threatened with the taint of shame.

Meantime our young men lift their eager gaze to the future, and are impatient of all that may seem to check or hinder their career. I sympathize with them. I wish them God-speed. They are the best dependence of Virginia, and in every· fibre of my being I thrill with their energy and gather inspiration from their hope.

But is this meeting of the Grand Army of the Republic a thing to be desired by the people of your city? Would your Confederate Camps be likely to forget their many repulses and cordially fraternize with these visitors? Would they entertain them with that free and effusive hospitality which has so long marked their treatment of the stranger within their gates? And failing this, even in slight degree, would not the day of healing be pushed further back?

As a separate proposition, perhaps nothing would be more instructive or more salutary than a close intermingling of our Southern youth with the men of the Grand Army. For the illusion which Northern literature has been fostering among our young people would be rather rudely dissipated when a mixed assemblage of these gentlemen should begin to regale you with their camp songs on "Marching Through Georgia," and the "Sour Apple Tree," and "Sheridan's Ride in the Valley." And to be less than prepared for this, would impose a restraint upon your guests which would rob their reunion of one of its striking characteristics.

As the Capital of the Confederacy—as

a city which withstood their beleaguering armies for four immortal years—Richmond would naturally be an object of interest to its captors, and I doubt not that these gentlemen would accept your invitation provided you could guarantee to them the customary fifty thousand dollars which they require for their entertainment.

But would it be well to thus utilize the memorials of a sorrowful and sacred past in the interests of a spectacle and a show? Would not the day of jubilee be a day of mourning to some of your noblest and most devoted people? Does not the historic fame of your fair city impose a class of obligations which you can not altogether disregard? And in any case would it not seem a little premature, and possibly in doubtful taste, to put yourselves in the position of proffering a forgiveness which has not been asked, and which might not even be desired?

In this connection I would recall the

BEFORE IT IS ASKED. 135

sentiments expressed some three years ago by a well-informed and patriotic Northerner. He said, in effect:

"If there is a more hopeless man than he who can neither forgive nor forget it is the 'chronic reconciler' who improves every opportunity to haul out his faded olive branch and wave it in the eyes of the people.

"The growth of reconciliation between the North and the South is the slow growth of years, and the work of generations. When any man, North or South, in a public place takes occasion to talk in a mellow and mawkish way of the great love he now has for his old enemy, watch him. He is getting ready to ask for something. There is a fine poetic idea in the reunion of two contending and shattered elements of a great nation. There is something beautifully pathetic in the picture of the North and the South clasped in each other's arms and shedding a torrent of hot tears down each other's backs as it is done in a play. But do you believe that the aged mothers on either side have learned to love the foe with much violence yet? Do you believe that the crippled veteran, North or South, now passionately loves the adversary who robbed him of his glorious youth, made him a feeble ruin, and mowed down his comrades with swift death? Do you believe that either warrior is so fickle that he has entirely deserted the cause for which he fought? Even the victor cannot ask that.

"Let the gentle finger of time undo, so far as may be, the devastation wrought by the war, and let succeeding generations seek by natural methods to reunite the business and the traffic which were interrupted by the conflict.

"Two warring parents on the verge of divorce have been saved the disgrace of separation and have agreed to maintain their household for the sake of their children. Their love has been questioned by the world, and their relations strained. Is it not bad taste for them to pose in public and make a cheap Romeo and Juliet tableau of themselves?

"Let time and merciful silence obliterate the scars of war, and succeeding generations, fostered by the smiles of natural prosperity soften the bitterness of the past and mellow the memory of a mighty struggle in which each contending host called upon Almighty God to sustain the cause which it honestly believed to be just.

"Let us be contented during this generation with the assurance that geographically the Union has been

BEFORE IT IS ASKED. 137

restored, and that each contending warrior has taken up the peaceful struggle for bettering and beautifying the home so bravely fought for." *

And let us not forget that to demand more than this, is to put in peril all that has been attained.

I fully join with you in the opinion that for Richmond or any other Southern city to assume the relation of host to an organization which is partly composed of negroes would at this time be peculiarly unfitting, and I sincerely hope that some other method may be devised for the advancement of Richmond's welfare.

With kindest regards, I am,
My dear Mr. Preston,
Sincerely yours,
JOHN CUSSONS.

---

*Nye's Hist. U. S.

ON THE "TREACHERY" OF THE AMERICAN INDIAN.

[From the Richmond (Va.) *Dispatch.*]

COL. CUSSONS DEFENDS THE INDIAN.

HIS STRIKING ADDRESS BEFORE THE WOMAN'S CLUB.

The members of the Woman's Club enjoyed a rare treat on Monday evening in the address delivered by Colonel John Cussons on the Indian. General Dabney H. Maury also made a bright and interesting little speech in presenting Colonel Cussons, who did not confine himself to the subject announced for the evening—"The Indian in Literature and Legend"—but spoke from his own experience in defence of the Red Man against the charges—cruelty, revengefulness, and treachery. The gallant ex-Confederate, who spent years on the frontier, spoke with great earnestness and vigor, and was heard with close attention and deep interest.

The chairman for the evening was Mrs. J. Arthur Lefroy, who, in a graceful manner, announced the speakers of the evening.

GENERAL MAURY'S SPEECH.

General Maury, after giving a witty illustration of his inability to make an extemporaneous speech, said:

"Your kindness in asking me to tell you about the North American Indians embarrasses me, for it is founded upon the belief that I know a great deal about those Indians, whereas, the fact is, that I know only what is bad in them, and it will be unfair to such unfortunate people to tell only what is bad in their nature. I share the sentiments of all men of the United States army whose official life has been passed in dealing with these, our natural enemies. For three hundred years we have known them only as malefactors of the most vengeful and cruel nature. We have taken from them their country, destroyed their homes, and hunted them down as beasts of prey. After generations of our people have been born and lived and died in this antagonism, it is no wonder that the brutal sentiment of one of the most ruthless of American commanders has found expression in the aphorism: 'There is no good Indian but a dead Indian.'

"As my observation of these unhappy people furnishes no exception to this verdict, I have been most fortunate in securing for your instruction this evening a gentleman who has probably observed and studied the Indian character more thoroughly than any man now living. My function, ladies, is to introduce to you our neighbor, Colonel John Cussons, who was for many years their guest and comrade—fought under Joe Johnston, Lee, and Forrest, and, after all his long experiences finally decided to become a Virginian and live amongst us. Permit me to introduce to you Colonel John Cussons, of Glen Allen, Virginia.

ADDRESS OF COLONEL CUSSONS.

Colonel Cussons was given a cordial reception. He said:

I was very glad, ladies, to hear General Maury's rebuke of the Sheridian aphorism that "there is no good Indian but a dead Indian," yet that pleasure was changed to surprise when he qualified his censure by directing it, not at the sentiment itself, but rather at "the ruthless commander" who uttered it.

The phrase is an effective one. It has been a comfort and a solace to us amid deeds which required palliation. And yet I am afraid that it is too flexible, too general in its application, to be accepted as a perfectly safe guide. As a recognized principle in casuistry it might prove awkward under changed conditions. Like Jeff Thompson's mountain howitzers it might do "great execution on the wrong side." What, for

THE AMERICAN INDIAN. 145

instance, if the Indian were to reverse the terms, and declare that "There is no good Yankee but a dead Yankee?" How would the sentiment strike us then? Should we feel that the phrase had settled the ethics of the case?—that the Indian would then be free to make "good people" of us? Or should we not probably change our views in the light of such practice? Might we not even go so far as to protest against the very principle itself?—the principle of setting up a rather sorry epigram as a substitute for the moral law?

And now I want to ask why it is that an illustrious and scholarly soldier, a brilliant essayist and able historian, a keen observer, and logical reasoner who has so abundantly demonstrated his fitness for discerning and depicting the life and character of one people, should so completely misinterpret the leading traits and characteristics of another people? For it may be justly said that if every other memorial of our epic period should perish, there would yet remain to us, in the "Recollections of a Virginian," a series of vivid pictures from which might be deduced the very form and pressure of the times. How, then, is it that the author of that volume—a volume which the philosophical historian of the future will justly regard as priceless—how is it that he who has painted so strikingly, with such felicity, and such fidelity, the life and spirit of the white American, should misread so strangely all the leading idiosyncracies of the red American?

An answer to this question would be a virtual solution of the most vexed feature of the Indian problem. And perhaps the easiest way to get a general grasp of the subject will be by running a few parallels on familiar lines.

It is evident that the relation which the Indian has borne to the white man on this continent resembles, in many respects, the relation which long existed between the people of the North and the people of the South. And it may be that, in the image of our cause we'll see the portraiture of his.

He was guilty, like ourselves, of possessing a goodly heritage, and was imbued with a strong desire to enjoy his own inheritance in his own way. Like ourselves, he was wedded to his own mode of life—the life of his fathers—and like us, he asked only to be let alone. Like ourselves, he was first wronged, until he resisted, and then crushed because he resisted. And, like ourselves, only in a greater degree, his story has been told by his enemy, and by his enemy alone. Like ourselves, in the process of subjugation, he has been judged by the apostates of his race; yet, with us, the apostates by this time have wellnigh run their course, while with him they still abide.

If we recall the evil days of Reconstruction, we shall have before us the conditions which confront the Indian still.

Our conquerors were inspired with a restless zeal to bring into the Union. fold all the lost spirits who had wandered into the desert places of Secessia. And when they had found such paragons of loyalty as Judge Underwood, or reclaimed such tristful penitents as Brother Hunnicut, they lifted up their voices and sang triumphant songs. Yet, when they had drawn the redeemed to their bosoms—when they began to catch the real flavor of their converts—it is little wonder that they marvelled exceedingly, and spake unto each other in shuddering whispers, saying: "If these are indeed the ransomed ones, what must the unregenerate be?"

And so, for a season, the renegade and the traitor and every creature which could crawl and writhe and betray acted after his kind, and received the wages of his apostacy. Yet in the fulness of time it was seen that back of these smooth and supraloyal proselytes were a great and earnest people, crushed to the dust, yet rich in every quality of a noble manhood. And so the hour of the scalawag passed away, and a new dawning opened upon the stricken South.

But with the Indian there was no change. The apostate continued to be his spokesman to the end, and the white man never realized that what he called the "friendly Indian" was always a traitor to his own people; an outcast, a sycophant, a hypocrite —in one word, a scalawag. These were the creatures, General, who appeared to army officers as the representatives of their race. It was these whom you employed as guides and scouts—the Hunnicuts of their tribes— false, uncleanly yahoos, with whom, perhaps, you would have to ratify solemn treaties; wretches who would sign away the domain of their people or commit any other infamy for a canteen of rum. Such were the "friendly" members of every independent or hostile tribe which ranged the plains in the old days which preceded their imprisonment on the reservations.

But glance down the shadowy past, and summon the free-born Lacotah of forty years ago—the indigenous native American, whom we have so wantonly destroyed. Look at him! Lithe, sinewy, strong, handsome in form, and in movement graceful as the leopard. Constant in his friendships, faithful to his people, crowned with the majesty which can dwell only where freedom is—a kingly bearing, tempered by that gracious courtesy which springs from a union of kindly feeling with conscious strength—these were the qualities which marked him while he remained untouched by our higher civilization. A savage he may have been—wild, unlettered, impatient

THE AMERICAN INDIAN. 151

of restraint—yet he had a devotion and a kindliness which were all his own; and I am not ashamed to say that I have met but few men who have more deeply impressed me with a sense of full manhood than the typical Lacotah warrior. It may be social treason to avow it, yet I have seen Robert E. Lee, both in bivouac and battle, when he has brought vividly to my mind the image of Matto-Num-Pa, a war chief of the Lacotahs.

These people were largely what their free life made them; a life of activity, often of hardship, never of routine toil. They drank in the fresh air of the desert, and all their physical surroundings were wholesome and pure. Their tribal fealty, their bond of brotherhood, was strengthened and close-knit by the presence of formidable enemies—Pawnees on the South, Utes on the west, and the white man steadily encroaching on their eastern border.

There were all the conditions among them of a full, material life; in some of its aspects fuller, and in most of its phases not less full than our own. No need of elaborate commerce or of manufactures. Their simple industry commanded the fruits which those activities yield. The buffalo was to them all, and more than all, that the reindeer is to the Laplander. It furnished them with food and clothing, with thread and cordage, with the lariat, the pishmore, and the lodge in which they dwelt. The pony represented almost universal uses. It was indispensable for war; indispensable for the chase. It was their measure of value, their medium of exchange. It stood for dowry, treaty, entertainment, currency, and transportation. Of the arts and sciences their knowledge was about equal to their needs. In jurisprudence they had the advantage of us, chiefly in this, that their laws were intelligible—even to those who studied them. They didn't worry themselves about tariffs, or fritter their lives away in trying to find out whether it was the producer or the consumer who paid the tax. They spent no strength on questions of bimetallism or monometallism. As I said, their currency was the pony, and they didn't care whether in was white or yellow, or even piebald, provided it would go.

But it is said that they are cruel, heartless, destitute of all emotion. Let us see. And let us not forget that the most ruthless cruelty is that which betrays through the affections.

I recall an incident which will illustrate my meaning.

Plainsmen of forty years ago will remember the old Frenchman, Provo, who had a ranch on the North Platte. He married an Ogalalla woman, and had the reputation of being the poorest shot in the country, although otherwise he was accounted a decent sort of a man. One day he picked up an antelope fawn and tethered it in a copse of willows about a mile from his lodge, and then went after his old Hawkins rifle, his idea being that the bleating of the fawn would attract the doe, and thus give him a pot shot. His squaw, suspecting what was going on, started for the river bottom on a dead run, and I cantered over to see what would happen. Wau-seech-ee Hung-Coo was a picture of rage and mortification. She seized his rifle and flung it in the slough, and then liberating the little fawn, and flipping her fingers at Provo, she stalked back towards the ranch, an embodyment of silent scorn. But soon she broke down, and signaling me to her side, she begged that I would forget the incident and never mention it to their children.

That "heathen women," General Maury, had never learned from us either the teachings or the deeds of mercy. No white man's lips had ever interpreted to her the divine injunction, "Thou shalt not seethe the kid in the mother's milk."

And now a word as to the revengeful character of these people. I think it is Mr. Blackstone who defines revenge as "a wild kind of justice." And with the Lacotahs, fair and equal reprisal certainly carried the sense of salutary and natural justice. It ranked with their highest virtues, and accompanied them—honor, courage, truth, self-devotion, fortitude, unshaken constancy.

We must remember that men may be beneath revenge, as well as above it. It is always easier to suffer a wrong than to redress it; it may or it may not be nobler. But it is at least certain that he who is swiftest in forgiving his enemies may be equally swift in forgetting his friends. Revenge relates to a personal wrong; justice to a public one. The injury which the Lacotah chiefly resented was not that which was done to himself, but to his tribe. It was not revenge, but simple justice.

But how about their treachery, their subtlety, their craft, their ineradicable deceit? That is supposed to have been their crowning infamy. It was that which made it our duty to blot them from the face of the earth. Well, take a few familiar examples. The so-called "Custer massacre," for instance. It was simply an attempted surprise met by a counter-surprise. Custer himself delivered the battle. The fight was in open field, and the numbers nearly equal. The Lacotahs simply outgeneralled, outmanœuvred, and outfought their adversaries. The only specific charge ever brought against them was that the "treacherous dogs" had armed themselves with rifles, "just like our own," when everybody knows that bows and arrows are the proper weapons for Indians.

The success of Sitting Bull's strategy turned on the chance that Custer's troops,

THE AMERICAN INDIAN. 157

on finding what appeared to be an undefended village, would make a reckless dash at it, and go to sabring the women and children; in which case an ambuscade ought not only to repulse their headlong charge, but should also impair their discipline, and break their ranks to such an extent that they might be scattered and beaten before they could effect a rally.

The old chief knew that Custer's Pawnee scouts had made a midnight reconnoissance of the village, and he had instructed his outposts not to molest them. He then prepared for the surprise party. Sending the women and children a few miles up the river, he supplied their places with a detachment of his warriors, ordering them to potter around the campfires and impersonate old women, cuddling little bundles of artificial babies, and keeping their rifles well hidden beneath their blankets. The moment the Long-Knives should come in sight they were to pick up the bundles and scuttle off, with every appearance of terror, toward the rising ground, where a number of others were to lie in ambush and join them in receiving the shock.

Note the situation, General, and let the charge of cruelty fall where it properly belongs. Sitting Bull risked everything—his lodges, his ponies, the stored wealth of his camp—on the single chance that his enemies would throw themselves into perilous disarray when afforded an opportunity to gratify what he deemed their innate savagery and sheer lust of blood.

Custer had received from his Pawnee scouts a full description of the situation, and was confident of a great victory. And so, in swift secrecy, he moved toward the tranquil village in the green valley of the Big Horn. As the trail led down to the ford, he divided his forces, so that none of the Indians might escape. The attacking column, believing itself undiscovered, got very near, and then, with headlong rush, swept to its prey. The imitation "squaws" fled in simulated terror towards the hills. The troopers dashed in their spurs! No longer riding boot to boot, but every horseman doing his best!—every sabre swirling—every eye gleaming—from every throat an exultant shout!

But just as they reached their intended victims the scene changes. With a swift movement, the "squaws" fling off their blankets, while all around them, from every turf and bush and rock, springs an armed warrior! The tables are turned! The ranks of death confront them! A gleam of painted faces, grim as fate, horrible as hell! a yell in their ears hideous as the blast of doom! the tremulous air quivering with the twang of arrows and the swirl of tomahawks and the flash of spears! The shock has appalled, dismayed, unnerved them! Men and horses crash down in a mass! The living steeds, with a snort of terror, recoil, and scatter over the plain. Swift pursuit is made. The fugitives reel in the saddle and tumble, one by one, clutching the empty air. A little remnant swims the river and joins the main body. And there, on Custer's chosen ground, the battle is fought to an end.

And then a cry of "Treachery" rings through all this land, and our moral sense demands a crusade of extermination!

"Treachery!" It is simply the interplay of ambuscade—of stroke and counterstroke —a vital element in the strategy of war.

But if this be indeed treachery, then the most treacherous man that ever planted foot on this round globe was Thomas Jonathan Jackson—our own thrice-glorious Stonewall. He was the very prince and potentate of deceivers—the quintessense of dissimulation.

See how he deceived poor Mr. Pope

during the three days and nights which led up to the Second Battle of Manassas. Why, he told that confiding general the most astounding lie that has ever been uttered in the universal sign-language of war—a lie sixty miles long! A tortuous, twisting, twining lie; a lie which worked its swift and sinuous course far up the south bank of the Rappahannock—doubling at Salem and White Plains—gliding across Hazel river; stealthily creeping behind the wall of Bull Run mountains; threading that range through Thoroughfare Gap, and then in the murk of midnight, swooping down on Bristow Station and Manassas Junction, and scattering commissaries and quartermasters and sutlers in a way that commissaries and quartermasters and sutlers had never been scattered before!

There he is—receiving railroad trains freighted with fresh supplies from Philadelphia and New York—but consigned to Mr.

Pope. All the riches of the world spread out before him—arms, munitions, blankets, shoes, bacon, flour, hardtack, coffee, canned goods—everthing that a soldier needs, world without end!

And where is Mr. Pope? He's out yonder at the front with seventy thousand men, covering the line of the Rappahannock from Kelly's Ford to Waterloo bridge. He had made his appointment to meet Jackson there; and Jackson knew it. Pope had announced to all the world that he didn't believe in fooling away time with "basis of supply" or "lines of retreat." Yet see how Jackson deceived him; striking him in the rear; destroying him; so twisting him up that he couldn't identify his own headquarters! Were Indians ever guilty of treachery more gross than that?

And see how he treated Shields, and Banks, and Hunter, and Milroy, and Fremont. He was everywhere except where those generals had a right to expect him!

Think of the trick he played on McClellan. When that able soldier had advanced his parallels to the very walls of this devoted city—just as the mailed hand of war was being stretched forth to clutch her—there was sudden tumult yonder, eight miles away, at Cold Harbor. Staff officers, in hot haste were dashing to McClellan's quarters, with news that the works were assailed; that the flank was turned; that the rebels were carrying all before them! Who stormed those ramparts? Who burst those barriers and hewed out the path to victory? It was that arch dissembler, Stonewall Jackson. What right had he on McClellan's flank, when McClellan and Lincoln and Stanton, and all the world believed him to be beyond the Blue Ridge mountains yonder, playing bo-peep with a trio of generals who were reporting two or three times a week that they had him surrounded at last, and would bag him on the morrow? Ah!

he was fearfully treacherous. There was no dependence to be placed in him—by the Federal commanders.

What was his conduct toward Hooker at Chancellorsville? Deceiving that General by a pretended retreat, he stealthily crept around his flank, and hurled such battle on the head of Fighting Joe as has no parallel in the annals of war. The Eleventh Corps (twenty thousand strong) passed from history on that fateful day. A fateful day, alas! for us, too, in the loss of that single life. But his fame is with the ages, now; his glory is the heritage of our race.

Let us have one weight and one measure. Let us be ashamed to call the same thing by different and contradictory names. Let the science of war, and its highest attribute, strategy, have the same name and the same honor, whether exercised by the white man or the red man. We see how incongruous is the charge of "treachery," when we impute it to that stainless soldier whose fame has filled the world. Why, then, should we apply the dishonoring word to a Lacotah chief, for the very acts and deeds, inspired by the self-same motives, which filled the heart and nerved the arm of Stonewall Jackson? Both alike fought for hearth and home, for ancient right, for the freedom which they had inherited from their fathers, for the freedom which they were bound, by every patriotic or tribal bond, to transmit unimpaired to their children.

If we had to kill those people, better that we had done it with open hand, like the robbers we are, than stain our souls by paltering with the truth—imputing to them the treachery which we ourselves have practiced.

And what are we that we should presume to draw an impassable line between our victims and ourselves?

Were not our own ancestors mere savages, but lately tamed? When civilization not less splendid than our own adorned all the coasts of the Mediterranean—when learning, and arts, and philosophies extended from the far Orient to the western sea—were not our fathers naked savages, living in caves and dens, devouring raw flesh, fighting for wives, and measuring strength with wild beasts? Are we not sprung from the loins of barbaric Britain, and marauding Dane, and free-booting Saxon? Does not the fierce blood of the old Norse sea kings flow in our veins?—that pirate brood who sailed the northern coasts, scattering in pale dismay the peaceful peoples, and ravaging every port where industry had made a foothold, or commerce had established a mart? Are we not proud to claim descent from the Norman robber, meaguer the bar-sinister across his 'scutcheon, thus conceding that we yield our homage to nothing but the mailed hand of force?

Would you have a more recent example? Turn back, then, for the brief period of three human lives, and you see a kindred people who were as wild, as untamed, as resentful of what we call civilizing influences as ever were the Lacotahs of the western plains. Mark the dying words of the typical Scottish Highlander, when he blessed his son and bade him remain true to the traditions of his fathers: "Plant no tree; build no house; dig not the soil. Keep thy refuge in the mountains. Spoil the invader who crosses thy border. Wear not the collar of the stranger. Be true to thy clansmen, and live the free life which thy fathers lived."

There are some tribes, some peoples, who can pass under the yoke; who can accept a master. There are others who can not— whose necks will not bend; whose souls can not yield. There must be time; time, and a change of circumstance. A little will suffice—a generation or two. It was enough for the Scot; it might have been enough for the Lacotah. The world can not afford to spill that adventurous, that unconquerable blood. The grandson of the old borderer has thrown aside the claymore, and to-day is leading the van of progress in all lands. To the Lacotah we gave no chance. We hunted him for our sport until we had lashed him into fury, and then turned loose upon him all the destructive "strength of civilization, without its mercy."

A final word on the fate of Sitting Bull, the gentle, kindly lad, who made his home with us in the lodge. His prestige as a prophet was due to his fixed conviction that sooner or later the white man would prove faithless. With his little band of followers he had kept the open field until about seven years ago, when, worn with battle-toil and civil care, he entered, at our urgent solicitation, into a treaty of permanent peace. He scrupulously observed the terms of his compact, and no accusation was ever brought against him, except that it was "believed" that he intended to leave the reservation. It was the first time that he had ever trusted us, and as soon as we had him completely within our power, in cold blood, we murdered him. That dark deed was committed under the auspices of a detachment of troops from Fort Yates, who had made a plot with the "Indian police" on the reservation. At a signal from the troops the police were to raise a disturbance, and thus get a pretext for the butchery. The disturbance failed, but the murder went on. It was at the dawn of a Sabbath morning that the troops, after a long night march, approached his camp. A cry was raised that the Long-Knives were coming; the idea being that he would either make a dash for his horse or stand on defence. He did neither. He bade his people be calm, telling them that they were in the hands of the Great White Chief, and that the Long-Knives were that chief's children. And so they had to stab him, as he stood in his tent, with his head bowed and his arms crossed upon his breast.

The deeds of Claverhouse were disavowed; as were those of Alva, and Aleric, and Dalrymple. We are less squeamish. The Massacre of Glencoe is still a stain on the government which condemned, yet did not avenge it. We are more practical. Before the desert breezes had lapped up the blood of this murdered chief we were mocking the "heathen moans" of his bereft kindred, and rejoicing in the fact that our holy religion had at last acquired supreme right of way.

And the Great White Chief (our late worthy President Mr. Benjamin Harrison) congratulated the country on this achievement, and assured us that the Indian question was a simple matter now that Sitting Bull had been put out of the way.

"Put out of the way" is a mild phrase. But, General Maury, you will pardon me for saying that it were better that ten thousand men should fall in the ranks of open battle, than that one life should be surreptitiously taken by connivance of the national authority.

My God!—Is it to this that our vaunted civilization has brought us at last?—that we, the children of light, the heirs of all the ages, should slay a confiding enemy whom our truce had beguiled, and then condone the crime by imputing to him a faithlessness which was all our own!

Have we, indeed, in dealing with these people, lost all sense of distinction between military strategy and personal treachery? Shall we take the sword of the soldier, which appeals in God's sunlight to earth and Heaven, and barter it for the stealthy dagger of the assassin?

In judging us as a nation, may the Almighty cast aside His scales of justice, lest He should deal with us as we have dealt with our unhappy victims.

These people, General Maury, were my friends. They were faithful and just to me, and in their behalf, on occasion, I will, at least, "unpack my heart with words."

www.ingramcontent.com/pod-product-compliance
Lightning Source LLC
Chambersburg PA
CBHW031451160426
43195CB00010BB/928